One Good Friend

One Good Friend

Illustrated by Becky Kelly

Written by Patrick Regan

**Andrews McMeel
Publishing**

Kansas City

ISBN: 0-7407-2087-2

02 03 04 05 06 LPP 10 9 8 7 6 5 4 3 2 1

Illustrations by Becky Kelly
Design by Stephanie Farley
Edited by Jean Lowe
Production by Elizabeth Nuelle

What a person needs most
in this weary old world
Isn't glory or wealth without end
But a comforting hand to hold on to
And the solace of one good friend.

It seems almost a miracle

That in the great world
we found each other.

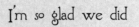

I'm so glad we did

And so lucky
to have a friend like you.

One good friend
who speaks with wisdom
and kindness,

And whispers reassuring words
when my belief wavers.

One good friend
who listens without judgment

And silently holds my hand
in moments when
no words are needed.

With one good friend
I have shared
a thousand silly giggles,

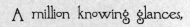
A million knowing glances,

And a handful of secret dreams
too precious to entrust
to anyone else.

One good friend has taught me
that no day
is more important than today.

That friendship holds the magical ability
to multiply joy
and divide sadness,

And most of all,

B. Kelly

One good friend has taught me
that sometimes one good friend
is all a person really needs.

You are to me,
as I am to you,

A calming influence
in a too-busy world,

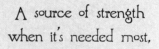

A source of strength
when it's needed most,

A wellspring of joy
when smiles are scarce,

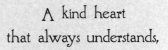

A kind heart
that always understands,

One good friend,
always.